AF126380

BOOK ANALYSIS

By Eli Cumings

Julius Caesar

BY WILLIAM SHAKESPEARE

BOOK ANALYSIS

BOOK ANALYSIS

Bright
≡Summaries.com

Fifty Shades
of Grey Trilogy
BY E. L. JAMES

Shed new light
on your favorite books with

Bright
≡Summaries.com

www.brightsummaries.com

WILLIAM SHAKESPEARE

ENGLISH PLAYWRIGHT AND POET

- **Born in Stratford-upon-Avon in 1564.**
- **Died in Stratford-upon-Avon in 1616.**
- **Notable works:**
  - *Venus and Adonis* (1593), poem
  - *Hamlet* (1603), play
  - *Macbeth* (1623), play

William Shakespeare is regarded as the most influential writer in English history. His 37 plays have been performed countless times, and have been reproduced and adapted across a broad range of periods and cultural contexts. As well as the plays, which can be loosely divided into tragedies, histories and comedies, Shakespeare wrote a number of narrative poems and sonnets. He also had an indelible influence on the English language itself, bringing a huge variety of words and phrases – as varied as "swagger", "bubble", "mind's eye" and "heart of gold" – into regular usage.

Shakespeare married Anne Hathaway in 1582 and had three children with her. Their only son, Hamnet, died at the age of 11. Very little else is known about Shakespeare's life, which he spent between Stratford-upon-Avon and London. It is clear, however, that his literary talents were matched by a shrewd entrepreneurial spirit. He made a number of profitable investments in his lifetime, which gave him the financial freedom to devote himself to acting and writing. In 1599, Shakespeare and his acting company (The Lord Chamberlain's Men) built the Globe Theatre on the banks of the River Thames in London. Many of Shakespeare's greatest plays were written to be performed at this theatre.

JULIUS CAESAR

A TRAGEDY IN FIVE ACTS

- **Genre:** play
- **Reference edition:** Shakespeare, W. (2008) *Julius Caesar*. London: Norton.
- **1st edition:** 1623
- **Themes:** power, ambition, tyranny, honour, revenge, freedom

The Tragedy of Julius Caesar portrays the lead up to and aftermath of the murder of Caesar, a respected and successful Roman leader on the verge of achieving absolute power. The men who conspire to murder him claim that they are saving Rome from a future of tyranny and oppression, but the reality is far less straightforward.

Although the play was not published until its inclusion in the First Folio of 1623, its first recorded performance was in 1599. Critics have speculated that the theme of tyranny might have resonated with an Elizabethan audience faced with the prospect of an ageing Queen showing no signs of relinquishing power to a husband or heir.

SUMMARY

A VICTORIOUS RETURN

Two Roman officials, Flavius and Murellus, come across a group of rejoicing tradesmen and reprimand them for not being at work. A cobbler explains that they are celebrating Caesar's victory over the sons of Pompey, a Roman general who had previously ruled alongside Caesar. Murellus is horrified to hear that a triumphal procession – usually reserved for victories over foreign adversaries – is being held to celebrate Caesar's victory over his own political enemies. He reminds the tradesmen that they once loved and admired Pompey, then instructs them to go home and pray for forgiveness. The two officials remove the decorations that the crowd had thrown over statues of Caesar.

Whilst Caesar celebrates with his wife and followers elsewhere in the city, a soothsayer calls out from the crowd warning him to "Beware the ides of March" (1.2.19). Caesar dismisses him as a "dreamer" (1.2.26) and departs to watch the races. Meanwhile, two Roman nobles called Cassius and Brutus engage in a conversation which is interrupted by the cheering crowd. Brutus worries that this cheering means that they have chosen Caesar as their king. Gaining confidence from Brutus's concern, Cassius begins to question Caesar's merit, asking why he is celebrated and treated as a god. Brutus promises to think about what Cassius has said, but declines to comment at present.

Returning from the races with his retinue, Caesar points out Cassius's "lean and hungry look" (1.2.195) to his closest friend – a man named Mark Antony. Antony speaks in Cassius's defence, pointing out that he is of noble birth. After Caesar and his train depart again, Casca – a friend of Cassius and Brutus – explains that Antony offered Caesar the crown three times, causing the crowd to burst into celebration. On each occasion Caesar declined and after the third refusal he fainted. Casca adds that Flavius and Murellus have been "put to silence" (1.2.280) for removing decorations from Caesar's statues. In the play's first soliloquy, Cassius reveals that he intends to manipulate Brutus and turn him against Caesar.

TROUBLING OMENS

Cicero, a Roman senator, comes across Casca standing stupefied in street in the middle of a violent storm. Casca reveals that he has witnessed both an earthquake and a tempest of fire, concluding that either there is a battle in Heaven, or the world is undergoing punishment for wronging the gods. He has also seen a lion walking the streets and a commoner with a burning, but unscathed, hand. Casca believes that these occurrences are prophetic, but Cicero argues that they can be interpreted in diverse ways by diverse people. After Cicero departs, Cassius arrives and reveals that he has been walking the streets with his jacket open, inviting the lightning to strike his chest. He interprets the storm as a sign that Caesar, who also thunders and roars, is actually nothing to be scared of. When Casca reveals that Caesar is likely to be crowned the next day, Cassius argues that their own complacency has enabled Caesar to become a tyrant. To reverse this trajectory, they must take the initiative and deliver themselves from servitude. Casca shares his perspective and they promise to support one another in the deliverance of Rome. Cassius instructs Cinna, another conspirator, to deliver a collection of letters to Brutus's house. We know from the earlier soliloquy that these letters are forgeries which celebrate Brutus's merits and subtly question Caesar's ascent to power.

Alone in his home, Brutus ponders the options before him. He has no personal grudge against Caesar, but believes his death would be beneficial to the common people. In the end, he decides that prevention is better than cure. Though Caesar has demonstrated no disturbing tendencies yet, he may be corrupted by the increased power. As Brutus confirms his decision, his servant Lucius appears with the first of the forged letters. Reading by the light of the meteors crowding the sky, Brutus finds his resolve strengthened by the letter, which demands that he "speak, strike, re-dress" (2.1.47). The conspirators arrive at Brutus's house, finalise their plans, and depart.

THE IDES OF MARCH

Caesar's wife Calpurnia seeks to dissuade her husband from attending the Capitol, as she has had a disturbing dream in which a group of Romans washed their hands in his blood. Though

Caesar initially dismisses this warning, along with similar warnings from his seers, he agrees to stay home as a personal favour to his wife. When another of the conspirators enters to accompany him to the Capitol, Caesar declines, giving Calpurnia's dream as the reason. Decius, however, argues that the dream is "a vision fair and fortunate" (2.2.84) and symbolises Rome's total dependency on Caesar. Furthermore, he adds that the senate intend to crown Caesar that day and that if he does not attend they may change their minds.

The action shifts to a street outside the Capitol where Artemidorus, a concerned supporter of Caesar, attempts to hand over a letter which warns him against the conspirators. The soothsayer from the opening of the play is also present, and warns Caesar that the ides of March are not yet over. Both warnings are ignored and Caesar and the conspirators move inside the Capitol. Caesar opens the proceedings and the conspirators approach and kneel before him. Then, one by one, they stab him. Brutus is the last to stab him, leading Caesar to ask "*Et tu, Bruté?*" (And you, Brutus?) (3.1.77). In the aftermath of the murder,

Antony arrives and speaks to the conspirators. He is devastated by Caesar's death, but agrees to reserve judgement until Brutus and the others have had a chance to explain their motivations. He asks to present Caesar's body to the public and to speak at his funeral. Brutus agrees despite Cassius's reservations.

TWO EULOGIES

Speaking at Caesar's funeral, Brutus is able to win over the commoners with an eloquent and balanced speech. He insists upon his love for Caesar and argues that the murder was committed in the interests of freedom: he was disturbed by Caesar's ambition and would rather kill one man to keep all Rome free, than risk the lives of all Romans by keeping Caesar alive. Happy with the outcome, Brutus steps down to make way for Antony and departs.

Antony's eulogy, however, is not supportive of the conspirators. He repeatedly calls them "honourable", with increasing sarcasm, and questions their portrayal of Caesar as ambitious. He argues that all Caesar did was for the good of the common people, then presents a will but refuses to read it. He relents after repeated requests, but asks that the assembled crowd gather by Caesar's corpse before he begins to read. After fanning the flames of anticipation even higher, Antony finally reads the will, revealing that Caesar has left his private gardens and a portion of his wealth to the public. The pro-Caesar sentiment reaches fever pitch and the commoners depart with Caesar's body, intending to riot.

THE BATTLE FOR REVENGE

The conspirators flee the city and Caesar's remaining supporters – Antony, Lepidus and Octavius – gather to make arrangements for rallying an army to defeat them in battle. Some time later, Cassius visits Brutus in his army's encampment and the pair argue over the treatment of one of the conspirators who has been taking bribes. They are able to reconcile with one another before the situation comes to blows, but Brutus reveals that his turbulent mental state is due to the fact that his wife Portia has recently committed suicide. After the others depart, Brutus has his servant play him some music, but the boy soon falls asleep. Caesar's ghost appears to

Brutus and tells him that they will meet again at Philippi – the site of the impending battle.

The two sets of commanders – Antony and Octavius, Brutus and Cassius – meet on the battlefield outside Philippi for a parley, but fail to reach a resolution. Deep into the battle, a soldier named Pindarus mistakenly reports that Titinus, an ally of Brutus and Cassius, is surrounded by Antony and Octavius's troops. Devastated by this news, Cassius demands that Pindarus stab him to death. Soon afterwards, Titinus arrives at the scene clad in a victory wreath and is devastated to come upon Cassius's corpse. He stabs himself and dies by Cassius's side.

As Antony's forces gain the upper hand in the battlefield, Brutus gathers the remainder of his allies and reveals that he has been visited by Caesar's ghost; he expects to die shortly. Realising the hopelessness of his situation and preferring death to dishonour, Brutus kills himself with the help of his friend Strato. Antony and his supporters find Brutus's body and discuss his virtues, describing him as the only conspirator who acted with the common good in mind. They agree that he should have an honourable burial and transport his body to their tents for safekeeping.

CHARACTER STUDY

CAESAR

Julius Caesar, the play's titular character, is a leader on the cusp of greatness. He has recently returned victorious from war and is beloved by the common people. He is a forthright and self-confident man, who is dismissive of unpalatable viewpoints and believes he has nothing to be afraid of. Though he instinctively distrusts Cassius, his pride overrules this fear and he declares: "I rather tell thee what is to be feared / Than what I fear, for always I am Caesar" (1.2.212-213).

Aside from this, he is something of an enigma. He has relatively few lines and is murdered a short way into Act 3. We are given very little sense of his hidden feelings and motivations. Much of what we know about him comes from the way he is described by other characters, and a very different picture of him emerges depending on who is speaking. Cassius, for example, remembers Caesar as a weak and frail man whom he was forced to save from the River Tiber. The devotion he inspires in his wife Calpurnia and his friend Antony, however, suggests a man with some redeeming qualities.

ANTONY

The noble Antony is lively and jovial, a fan of plays, music and sport. He is trusting by nature and dismisses Caesar's suspicions of Cassius early in the play. After the murder he becomes more devious, successfully gaining the trust of the conspirators in order to put his plans for revenge into action. His address to the common people is also incredibly devious. He utilises reverse psychology, repeatedly urging the assembled group *not* to riot or to avenge Caesar, and is clearly well aware of the dramatic potential of Caesar's mutilated body and bleeding wounds. Though he is relentless in his pursuit of revenge, he remains sympathetic to Brutus until the very end, describing him as "the noblest Roman of them all" (5.5.67).

BRUTUS

Brutus is a member of the nobility and a trusted friend of Caesar's. Brutus is motivated primarily by honour: "I love / The name of honour more than I fear death" (1.2.90-91). When Cassius attempts to win Brutus over with flattery, he responds in a measured manner and carefully weighs up his options with the good of the common people in the forefront of his mind. Brutus also wields a great amount of authority with the conspirators; though he is a later addition to their group, he dominates the discussion and forcefully rejects a number of suggestions. For example, when Cassius suggests that they swear an oath to achieve their aim Brutus disagrees, arguing that swearing is for priests, cowards and weaklings.

After the murder, Brutus recommends a course of transparency and honesty: he is the one who suggests that they bathe their hands in blood and boldly proclaim their act. Brutus also decides that Antony should be permitted to speak at the funeral, believing that the integrity of their motivations will be evident and that Antony's speech can only add credibility to their actions. Brutus continues to advocate for the most direct routes during the civil conflict, when he decides that they will march into battle and face the enemy directly, rather than lying in wait and hoarding resources as Cassius suggests. However, his resolve begins to crumble after the news of his wife's suicide and his first sighting of Caesar's ghost. When he eventually commits suicide with the help of Strato he gains some measure of peace, saying: "Caesar, now be still. / I killed not thee with half so good a will" (5.5.50-51).

PORTIA

Brutus's wife Portia is an intelligent, strong-willed woman who is very attentive to her husband's mood and disposition. She is reminiscent of Lady Macbeth in her desire for power and her disdain for her womanhood: "I have a man's mind, but a woman's might. / How hard it is for women to keep counsel!" (2.4.8). When she believes Brutus is hiding something from her she compellingly argues the case for her inclusion, demonstrating a self-inflicted wound as proof of her resolve. Unlike Calpurnia, who is unable to convince Caesar to stay at home, Portia is successful in convincing her husband to make her privy to his plans. She struggles with the news, however, debating whether to send a servant to the Capitol to intervene.

CASSIUS

Though Caesar describes the nobleman Cassius as a shrewd and serious observer who is uninterested in the pleasures of games and entertainments, he is no fusty academic. His bravery is repeatedly demonstrated, whether through jumping into the freezing Tiber, bearing his chest to a lightning storm, or initiating a bloody coup. Cassius is also a compelling speaker who utilises different persuasive techniques depending on his target. In order to win over Brutus, for example, Cassius repeatedly refers to the will of the people. On the other hand, he convinces Casca of the legitimacy of his enterprise by linking it to superstition and portents.

Cassius is also an insightful reader of other people who is wary enough to correctly guess at the hidden motivations of others. After the murder, he is rightfully suspicious of Antony and does not want him to speak at the funeral. His wariness also extends to his military tactics. Before the battle, he suggests drawing their opponents out and forcing them to waste their resources, rather than marching to meet them in battle. In both cases, however, Cassius defers to Brutus. In the end, Cassius dies a rather anti-climactic death resulting from a misunderstanding.

ANALYSIS

GENRE

Though *The Tragedy of Julius Caesar* focuses on historical figures, it is not a 'history play' in the Shakespearean sense. Shakespearean history plays, like *Richard III* (1597) or *Henry V* (1600), deal specifically with English history and English monarchs. As the play's full title suggests, *Julius Caesar* is a tragedy.

Caesar plays a surprisingly minimal role in the play, however; he dies a short way into Act 3 and has relatively few lines. Caesar is the victim of the tragedy rather than its hero, his death inspiring Antony's revenge and prompting Brutus's downfall from nobility to defeat and suicide.

The play also has a number of other features characteristic of Shakespearean tragedy, which include:

- a public focus – the action concerns the leadership of Rome, rather than a domestic issue;

- comic relief, including witty wordplay;
- a bloody ending.

PUBLIC OPINION

The common people, or "base degrees" (2.1.26), have a pivotal role in the play and are at the centre of its opening scene. They adore Caesar, a fact which does not endear them to the conspirators. Describing Caesar's refusal of the crown, for example, Casca says:

> "And still as he refused it, the rabblement hooted, and clapped their chapped hands, and threw up their sweaty nightcaps, and uttered such a deal of stinking breath because Caesar refused the crown that it had almost choked Caesar; for he swooned and fell down at it." (1.2.242-246)

Their impassioned support for Caesar marks them out as targets for ridicule, and Casca pays particular attention to their filthy and impoverished state. With its emphasis on hooting and clapping, this comment also gestures to the audience of the play itself. The comparison, however, is not flattering.

Other characters are more sympathetic towards the common people, or at least aware of the power they wield. In the aftermath of Caesar's death, both Brutus and Antony attempt to win them over with lengthy and considered speeches. Their strategies are successful, as the commoners are swayed first one way and then the other. Again, the commoners represent an audience of sorts: they observe the performances by Brutus and Antony and provide a running commentary on them.

READING THE SIGNS

The play is filled with thunderstorms, meteor showers and blazing fires. This is typical of Shakespearean tragedies, in which dramatic and horrible actions – particularly regicide – are frequently anticipated by exceptional natural events: "When beggars die there are no comets seen; / The heavens themselves blaze forth the death of princes" (2.2.30-31). Another notable portent is the appearance of the ghost of Caesar, which Brutus takes to symbolize his defeat in battle, then his death. The play, however, destabilizes the notion of easily legible signs. As Cicero observes, portents can be interpreted variously depending on who is reading them. For example, when Calpurnia warns Caesar against attending the Capitol, citing the fact that a recently sacrificed bull had no heart, Caesar argues that this is a warning against cowardice.

FURTHER REFLECTION

SOME QUESTIONS TO THINK ABOUT...

- Are the conspirators justified in killing Caesar? Is there any evidence from the play to support or contradict their fears of tyranny?
- Pick out two characters and compare their attitudes towards the common people. How does this reflect on their attitudes more generally?
- Who, aside from Brutus, could be regarded as the play's tragic hero? What are their flaws?
- Look closely at Act 2 Scene 4. What does this scene tell us about Portia and how does it match up with her portrayal elsewhere?
- The play contains a number of short scenes (2.3, 3.3 and 5.2, for example). What is the purpose of these scenes and how do they affect the pace of the play?
- How would you stage the murder scene? Think about the positioning of the individual characters and their movement across the stage.

- How does the ghost of Caesar compare to the ghosts in *Macbeth* and *Hamlet*? Why does Shakespeare choose to include a ghost of this kind?
- At the close of the play, Antony describes Brutus as "the noblest Roman of them all" (5.5.67). Do you agree?

We want to hear from you!
Leave a comment on your online library
and share your favourite books on social media!

FURTHER READING

REFERENCE EDITION

- Shakespeare, W. (2008) *Julius Caesar*. London: Norton.

REFERENCE STUDIES

- Ballard, K. (2016) Rhetoric, power and persuasion in Julius Caesar. *British Library*. [Online]. [Accessed 15 November 2018]. Available from: <https://www.bl.uk/shakespeare/articles/rhetoric-power-and-persuasion-in-julius-caesar>

- Cooper, M. (2017) Why 'Julius Caesar' Speaks to Politics Today. With or Without Trump. *New York Times*. [Online]. [Accessed 15 November 2018]. Available from: <https://www.nytimes.com/2017/06/12/theater/julius-caesar-shakespeare-donald-trump.html>

ADAPTATIONS

- *Julius Caesar*. (1953) [Film] Joseph L. Mankiewicz. Dir. United States: Metro-Goldwyn-Mayer.

MORE FROM BRIGHTSUMMARIES.COM

- Reading guide – *Antony and Cleopatra* by William Shakespeare.

- Reading guide – *Hamlet* by William Shakespeare.

- Reading guide – *King Lear* by William Shakespeare.

- Reading guide – *Macbeth* by William Shakespeare.

- Reading guide – *Measure for Measure* by William Shakespeare.

- Reading guide – *The Merchant of Venice* by William Shakespeare.

- Reading guide – *A Midsummer Night's Dream* by William Shakespeare.

- Reading guide – *Much Ado About Nothing* by William Shakespeare.

- Reading guide – *Othello* by William Shakespeare.

- Reading guide – *Richard III* by William Shakespeare.

- Reading guide – *Romeo and Juliet* by William Shakespeare.

- Reading guide – *The Tempest* by William Shakespeare.

- Reading guide – *Titus Andronicus* by William Shakespeare.

- Reading guide – *Twelfth Night* by William Shakespeare.

- Reading guide – *The Two Gentlemen of Verona* by William Shakespeare.

Bright ≡Summaries.com

More guides to rediscover your love of literature

Animal Farm
BY GEORGE ORWELL

The Stranger
BY ALBERT CAMUS

Harry Potter and the Sorcerer's Stone
BY J.K. ROWLING

The Silence of the Sea
BY VERCORS

Antigone
BY JEAN ANOUILH

The Flowers of Evil
BY BAUDELAIRE

www.brightsummaries.com

Although the editor makes every effort to verify the accuracy of the information published, BrightSummaries.com accepts no responsibility for the content of this book.

© BrightSummaries.com, 2019. All rights reserved.

www.brightsummaries.com

Ebook EAN: 9782808015714

Paperback EAN: 9782808015721

Legal Deposit: D/2018/12603/544

Cover: © Primento

Digital conception by Primento, the digital partner of publishers.